CW01667594

International Thai Cooking

DELICIOUS THAI CUISINE

Sangdad Publishing Co., Ltd.
Bangkok, Thailand

National Library of Thailand Cataloging in Publication Data
Delicious Thai Cuisine.--4th ed.--Bangkok : Saengdad, 2001.
104 p.
1. Cookery, Thai. I. Title.
641.5
ISBN 974-7163-01-2

Saengdad Books
Published by Saengdad Publishing Co., Ltd.
320 Lat Phrao 94 (Town in Town)
Wangthonglang, Bangkok 10310, Thailand.
Tel. (662) 538-7576, 538-5553, 934-4414
Fax : (662) 538-1499
e-mail : sdbooks@sangdad.com

First published 1994 by Saengdad Publishing Co., Ltd.
Second published 1998 by Saengdad Publishing Co., Ltd.
Third published 1998 by Saengdad Publishing Co., Ltd.
Fourth published 2001 by Saengdad Publishing Co., Ltd.
Copyright © 1994 by Saengdad Publishing Co., Ltd.
Photographs Copyright © 1994 by Saengdad Publishing Co., Ltd.

All rights reserved. No part of this book may be reproduced or utilized in any forms or by any means, electronic or mechanical without prior written permission of the publisher.

Consultant : Sisamon Kongpan
Director : Nidda Hongwiwat
Editor : Nalin Khu-Armornpatana
English editor : Richard Goldrick
Editor's Assistant : Obchery Imsabai
Photography : Samart Sudto
Design : Samart Sudto
Lay Out : Rungrudee Panichsri
Illustration : Sarayut Yoosuk
Marketing Director : Waynisa Chotiaroon
Production Director : Jiranun Tubniem
Printer : Pimdee Co., Ltd. Tel. (662) 803-2694-7

PREFACE

Because Thai food is delicious, nutritious, and easy to cook, it is becoming more and more popular internationally and winning a well-deserved place in global culinary culture. In keeping with this globalization of Thai food, the Recipe Development Section of Sangdad, the biggest publisher of cookbooks in Thailand, has compiled a collection of over 5,000 recipes for traditional Thai and contemporary Thai-style dishes, and now presents a selection of these in the Easy Cooking Series.

The editor of this volume, Nalin Khu-Armornpattana, has carefully studied the preferences of the many international admirers of Thai food, and so *Delicious Thai Food* contains a fine collection of favorites which are both appetizing and easy to prepare.

With *Delicious Thai Food* and a little practice, you can make in your own home the Thai dishes you and your loved ones like best.

Nidda Hongwiwat
Managing Director

INTRODUCTION

One of the secrets of Thai cooking is the use of spices. Here ingerdients including spices used in our recepies are listed. Eash will be briefly described, and its Thai name listed. It is hoped that wanted ingredients in the market.

ANIMAL PRODUCTS

Mackerel, pla thu, **ปลาทู,** is a small saltwater fish, *Rastrelliger chrysozonus* (Scombridae). Steamed mackerel in small woven trays are sold in food shops nearly everywhere in the country ; **fresh mackerel,** pla thu sot, **ปลาทูสด,** are available at the fish-monger's in the market.

White pomfret is pla jalamet khao, **ปลาจะละเม็ดขาว,** *Pampus argenteus,* also known in English as grey or silver pomfret, silver or white butter fish, pompano, and spadefish.

Serpent head, pla chon, **ปลาช่อน,** is the freshwater fish *Ophiocephalus striatus.*

Sea perch, pla kaphong, **ปลากะพง,** is a general name for fish of the sea bass and sea perch families.

Rock cod, pla kao, **ปลาเก๋า,** is also known as grouper, reef cod, and sea bass.

The **white prawn,** kung chaebuai, **กุ้งแชบ๊วย,** also called the banana prawn, has a white body stippled with minute dots of rust-colored pigment. Fully grown, these prawns attain a length of 20 cm and more ; however, harvesting may begin before they have reached half this. These smaller ones, sorted and priced by size, are sold as kung chihae, **กุ้งชีแฮ้,** which in the recipes are designated simply as prawns.

The **spiny-clawed prawn,** kung kam kram, กุ้งก้ามกราม, known also as the giant freshwater prawn, in nature begins life in the brackish water of river mouths and then moves up-stream. The second walking leg on each side is extremely long and ends in a large pincer studded with spines, hence the name. Spiny-clawed prawns whose entire bodies are blue are more tender when broiled or baked than those which are grey-green.

Crispy fried pork skin, Khaep mu is made by removing most–but not all–of the fat from fresh pork skin and then rubbing the skin with salt and then boiling in water. The skin is drained, and then spread out on the inner surface of a wok and soaked in oil for two days. After this, the skin is placed in hot sunlight for one day and then deep fried in very hot oil until it puffs up and becomes crispy.

SEASONING SAUCE

Fish sauce, nam pla, น้ำปลา, is a clear, brown liquid derived from a brew of fish or shrimp mixed with salt. It is sold in bottles and plastic jugs as well as in earthenware jars. High quality fish sauce has a fine aroma and taste. Fish sauce is placed on the table as a condiment at nearly every meal, either as is or mixed with sliced chillies and perhaps lime juice.

Chilli fish sauce, nam pla phrik ma-nao , น้ำปลาพริกมะนาว, is made by mixing 2 tablespoonsful of fish sauce, 2 teaspoonsful of lime juice, and 1 teaspoonsful of chillies. It is used as a sauce to accompany fried foods or as a condiment with rice.

Oyster sauce, nam man hoi, น้ำมันหอย, is a sweetened soy sauce to which oyster extract is added.

Soybean paste, tao jiao nam, เต้าเจี้ยวน้ำ, is a preparation made with fermented soybeans and flour.

Light soy sauce, si-iu khao, ซีอิ๊วขาว, is a clear brown liquid used in much the same way that fish sauce is.

Dark soy sauce, si-iu dam, ซีอิ๊วดำ, is opaque, black, viscous, and sweet. It is mixture of soy sauce and molasses.

Roasted chilli sauce, nam phrik phao , น้ำพริกเผา, is a mixture of chillies, shallots, garlic, dried shrimp, and palm sugar which is stir fried until fragrant. It can be bought in markets and supermarkets or can be made at home. It can be spread on bread, mixed with rice.

Shallot หอมเล็ก

Garlic กระเทียม

Nut meg and Mace ลูกจันทน์, และดอกจันทน์

Chillies พริก

Ginger ขิง

Galangal ข่า

Ripe Tamarind มะขามเปียก

Parched rice ข้าวคั่ว

Bitter gourd มะระ

Swamp cabbage ผักบุ้ง

Celery ขึ้นฉ่าย

Sponge gourd บวบเหลี่ยม

Phak chi farang ผักชีฝรั่ง

Bell Chilli พริกหยวก

Mint leaves สะระแหน่

Lemon grass ตะไคร้

Tamarind juice, nam som ma-kham, **น้ำส้มมะขาม,** is obtained by mixing some of the ripe fruit with water and squeezing out the juice.

Curry powder, phong ka-ri, **ผงกะหรี่,** is a prepared mixture of spices such as turmeric, coriander seed, ginger, cloves, cinnamon, mustard, cardamom, cumin, chilli, and salt. Each brand has its own character depending on the ingredients used.

HERBS AND SPICIES

Nut meg and Mace, luk jan and dawk jan, **ลูกจันทน์ และดอกจันทน์** Nutmeg is a dark brown, egg-shaped seed and mace is the yellowish brown, petal-like covering of the seed.

Garlic, kra-thiam, **กระเทียม.** Thai garlic has small cloves covered with a peel that is not tough. Its fragrance is stronger than that of large-cloved garlic. In making fried garlic, the peel is usually not removed entirely so that only the flesh remains. Some of the peel is left on the clove, for it is in the peel that the fragrance resides.

Coriander, phak chi, **ผักชี,** *Coriandrum sativum,* is of the parsley family. The leaves and stems are eaten fresh and used frequently as a garnish. The root and the seeds are ingredients in many dishes.

Phak chi farang, ผักชีฝรั่ง, is a plant with long, narrow leaves, measuring about 3-4 inches long and about 1/2 inch across. The margins of the leaf are toothed. Phak chi farang is used in savory meat salads *(lap)* and is also a fragrance all these dishes. It has eaten fresh with its own.

Ginger, khing, **ขิง,** *Zingiber officinale,* grows from an underground stem, or rhisome. Mature ginger stems are buff colored ; young or fresh ginger, khing on, **ขิงอ่อน,** is white and is eaten fresh and pickled as well as cooked.

Galangal, kha, **ข่า,** *Alpinia galangal,* is a largar and lighter-colored relative of ginger and has its own distinctive taste.

Mint leaves, sa-ra-nae, **สะระแหน่.** Thai mint leaves are round, not thick, hairless, and slightly wavy. The stem tends to be dark red. It is easy to grow, and Thais commonly plant it in pots kept near the kitchen, where it can always be easily gathered.

Lemon grass, ta-khrai, **ตะไคร้,** *Cymbopgon citratus,* is an aromatic grey-green grass. The bases of the stems are used in cookery.

Shallot, hom lek, **หอมเล็ก,** or hom daeng, **หอมแดง,** *Allium ascalonicum,* is the zesty small red onion favored in Thai cooking.

Kaffir lime, ma-krut, **มะกรูด,** Citrus hystrix, has green fruits with wrinkled skin. The rind and the leaves are used in cookery.

Chillies, phrik, **พริก,** *Capsicum annuum,* of several varieties are available in Thailand. As they ripen, they change color from green to red and become hotter. Fully ripe fruits are dried in the sun to give **dried chillies,** phrik haeng, พริกแห้ง pounded for ground dried chilli, **bell chilli,** phrik yuak, พริกหยวก, is light green in color and mild in taste. They are used in spicy salads and chilli pastes for their fragrance, and in stir-fried meat dishes for both flower and aroma.

Water mimosa, phak ka-chet, **ผักกระเฉด,** *Neptunia oleracea,* has small dark green compound leaves and a smooth green stem encased in a white foamlike material which is stripped off before use.

Swamp cabbage, phak bung , **ผักบุ้ง,** *Ipomoea aquatica,* also called water convolvulus, water spinach, or aquatic morning glory, has hollow stems and roughly triangular leaves.

Kale, phak kha-na, **ผักคะน้า,** *Brassica oleracea* (acephala variety), has leathery grey-green leaves on thick stalks.

Sponge gourd, buap liam, **บวบเหลี่ยม,** *Luffa acutangula,* also called vegetable gourd or Chinese okra, is oblong, pointed, and dark green and has sharp longitudinal ridges.

Bitter gourd, ma-ra, **มะระ,** *Momordica charantia,* also called bitter cucumber, carilla fruit, or balsam pear, is an oblong fruit, pointed at one end, which has a handsome pale green surface covered with an irregular pattern of ridges.

Spring onion, ton hom **ต้นหอม,** *Allium fistulosum,* also called green onion or scallion, has leaves that are circular in cross section.

Garlic plant, ton kra-thiam, **ต้นกระเทียม,** *Allium sativum,* is the young plant picked before the bulb has formed. The leaves are flat and folded length-wise.

Celery, kheun chai, **ขึ้นฉ่าย,** *Apium graveolens,* also called celeriae, tuniprooted celery, or Chinese soup celery, has very small stalks(only a few millimeters across)and a very strong flower.

TABLE OF CONTENTS

Yam Pla Thu

Spicy mackerel salad

ยำปลาทู

Ingredients

5 large short-bodied mackerels
10-15 broken hot chillies
7 finely sliced shallots
1/2 cup shredded young ginger
5 finely slice lemon grass stems
2 tbsp. finely sliced kaffir lime leaves
1 cup horapha sweet basil leaves
2 tbsp. ground roasted peanuts
2-3 tbsp. lime juice
2 tbsp. fish sauce
fresh vegetables : Chinese cabbage, yard-long beans, cabbage, spring onions, coriander greens

Preparation

1. Fry the mackerel golden brown and remove the meat.
2. Toss with the meat the lemon grass, ginger, shallot, chillies, kaffir lime leaf, sweet basil leaves, fish sauce, and lime juice.
3. Just before serving, sprinkle with the ground peanut, and serve with the fresh vegetables.

เครื่องปรุง

ปลาทูตัวใหญ่	๕	ตัว
พริกขี้หนูบุบ	๑๐-๑๕	เม็ด
หอมแดงซอย	๗	หัว
ขิงอ่อนซอย	๑/๒	ถ้วย
ตะไคร้หั่นฝอย	๕	ต้น
ใบมะกรูดหั่นฝอย	๒	ช้อนโต๊ะ
โหระพาเด็ดเป็นใบ	๑	ถ้วย
ถั่วลิสงคั่ว	๒	ช้อนโต๊ะ
น้ำมะนาว	๒-๓	ช้อนโต๊ะ
น้ำปลา	๒	ช้อนโต๊ะ

ผักสด ผักกาดขาว ถั่วฝักยาว กะหล่ำปลี ต้นหอม ผักชี

วิธีทำ

1. ทอดปลาทูให้สุกเหลือง ตักขึ้น แกะเอาแต่เนื้อปลาทู
2. ใส่ตะไคร้หั่นฝอย ขิงอ่อนซอย หอมแดงซอย พริกขี้หนูบุบ ใบมะกรูดหั่นฝอย ใบโหระพา น้ำปลา น้ำมะนาว เคล้าให้เข้ากัน
3. เวลาเสิร์ฟ โรยถั่วลิสง รับประทานกับผักสด

Yam Khaep Mu

Crisp pork skin salad

ยำแคบหมู

Ingredients

1 cup thinly sliced crisp-fried pork skin
1 tsp. kaffir lime leaves, sliced into thin strips
1 dried chilli
1 tbsp. crisp fried shallot slices
1 garlic bulb
1 tsp. salt
1 tsp. fish sauce
1 tsp. lime juice

Preparation

1. Wash the chilli and garlic and then roast. Peel the garlic, and then pound it together with the chilli and salt until finely ground.
2. Mix the ground chilli and garlic, fish sauce, lime juice, with the pork skin, transfer to a serving dish, sprinkle with the fried shallot, kaffir lime leaves.

เครื่องปรุง

แคบหมูหั่นบาง	1 ถ้วย
ใบมะกรูดหั่นฝอย	1 ช้อนชา
พริกแห้ง	1 เม็ด
หอมแดงเจียว	1 ช้อนโต๊ะ
กระเทียม	1 หัว
เกลือป่น	1 ช้อนชา
น้ำปลา	1 ช้อนชา
น้ำมะนาว	1 ช้อนชา

วิธีทำ

1. ล้างพริกแห้ง กระเทียม เผาไฟให้สุก ปอกเปลือกกระเทียม แล้วโขลกรวมกับพริกและเกลือให้ละเอียดเข้ากันดี
2. ตักเครื่องที่โขลกผสมกับแคบหมู น้ำปลา น้ำมะนาว คนให้เข้ากัน ตักใส่จาน โรยหน้าด้วยหอมเจียว และใบมะกรูด

Yam Pla Meuk

Spicy squid salad

ยำปลาหมึก

Ingredients

500 grams squid or cuttlefish
1/4 cup shredded young ginger
1 cup mint leaves
1 cup Chinese soup celery cut into 1-inch lengths
1 red spur chilli sliced lengthwise
1 cup thinly sliced onion

Preparation

1. Wash and eviscerate the squid or cuttlefish and remove the eyes. If using squid, skin them. Score the bodies in a crisscross pattern and then cut into 1 1/2-inch pieces.
2. Scald the squid or cuttlefish in boiling water for just a short time. Overly long scalding will make them tough.
3. Toss together with the squid or cuttlefish the onion, ginger, celery, and dressing. Taste and adjust the seasoning as required.
4. Transfer to a bed of mint arranged upon a plate and sprinkle with red chilli.
5. Dressing : pound the 2-3 hot chillies and 2 tbsp. sliced garlic until finely ground and then mix with 1/4 cup lime juice and 3-4 tbsp. fish sauce.

เครื่องปรุง

ปลาหมึก	๕๐๐ กรัม
ขิงอ่อนซอย	1/4 ถ้วย
สะระแหน่เด็ดใบ	1 ถ้วย
ขึ้นฉ่ายตัดท่อนยาว 1 นิ้ว	1 ถ้วย
พริกแดงหั่นฝอยแต่งหน้า	1 เม็ด
หอมใหญ่หั่นตามขวางบาง ๆ	1 ถ้วย

วิธีทำ

1. ล้างปลาหมึกชักไส้และเอาตาออก ถ้าเป็นปลาหมึกกล้วย ลอกหนังออก ใช้มีดกรีดบั้งเป็นตาตาราง หั่นเป็นชิ้นเล็ก ๆ ขนาด 1 1/2 นิ้ว
2. ต้มน้ำให้เดือด ลวกปลาหมึกเร็ว ๆ ถ้าลวกนานจะแข็งเหนียว ตักขึ้น
3. ผสมปลาหมึก หอมใหญ่ ขิงซอย ขึ้นฉ่าย เคล้าเบา ๆ ชิมรส
4. จัดสะระแหน่รองจาน ตักยำใส่จาน โรยพริกแดง
5. น้ำยำ โขลกกระเทียมหั่น 2 ช้อนโต๊ะ พริกขี้หนู 2-3 เม็ดให้ละเอียดผสมกับน้ำมะนาว 1/4 ถ้วย น้ำปลา 3-4 ช้อนโต๊ะ

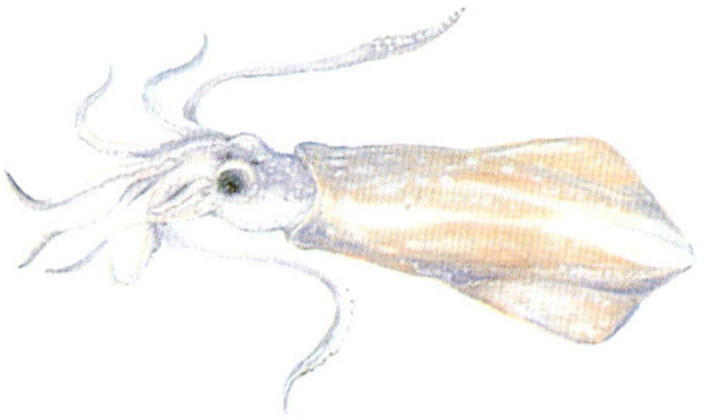

Kung Op Rot Det

Spicy Baked Prawns

กุ้งอบรสเด็ด

Ingredients

1 kilogram spiny-clawed prawns or tiger prawns
1 1/2 tbsp. pounded tiny hot chillies
3-4 garlic bulbs
1 tsp. ground pepper
1 1/2 tsp. salt
1 tsp. cooking oil

Preparation

1. Wash the prawns, split open along the back and remove the dark vein, and then deepen the cut to about halfway through the prawn.
2. Pound the garlic, pepper, chillies, and salt until throughly ground, remove from the mortar, and mix with the oil.
3. Fill the cuts in the backs of the prawns with this mixture, and rub it over the bodies of the prawns as well.
4. Bake the prawns in an oven at 350° F. Serve immediately when done with the cabbage.

เครื่องปรุง

กุ้งก้ามกราม หรือกุ้งกุลาดำ	1	กิโลกรัม
พริกขี้หนูโขลก	1 1/2	ช้อนโต๊ะ
กระเทียม	3-4	หัว
พริกไทยป่น	1	ช้อนชา
เกลือป่น	1 1/2	ช้อนชา
น้ำมัน	2	ช้อนโต๊ะ

วิธีทำ

1. ล้างกุ้งให้สะอาด ผ่าหลังชักเส้นดำออก ผ่าหลังให้ลึกเกินครึ่งตัว
2. โขลกกระเทียม พริกไทย พริกขี้หนู เกลือให้ละเอียด ตักขึ้นผสมน้ำมัน
3. นำเครื่องที่โขลกใส่หลังกุ้งที่ผ่า และเอาตัวกุ้งคลุกเคล้ากับเครื่องด้วย
4. อบกุ้งด้วยไฟ 350° ฟ. พอสุกตักออกเสิร์ฟร้อน ๆ กับกะหล่ำปลี

Kung Ten

Spicy broiled prawns

กุ้งเต้น

Ingredients

3 large spiny-clawed prawns
1 head lettuce, sliced into strips
2 tbsp. chopped hot chillies
2 tbsp. chopped garlic
1 small coriander plant
2 tbsp. lime juice
1 1/2 tbsp. fish sauce

Preparation

1. Wash and shell the prawns and remove the sack-like stomach from behind the mouth. Broil until just slightly done ; then, split each in half and place upon a bed of lettuce arranged on a platter.
2. Mix the garlic and chillies with the fish sauce and lime juice ; the taste should be hot, sour, and salty, but may be varied as desired. Pour the sauce over the prawns, garnish with coriander greens, and serve.

เครื่องปรุง

กุ้งนางตัวใหญ่	3	ตัว
ผักกาดหอมหั่นเป็นท่อน	1	ต้น
พริกขี้หนูสับ	2	ช้อนโต๊ะ
กระเทียมสับ	2	ช้อนโต๊ะ
ผักชี	1	ต้นเล็ก ๆ
น้ำมะนาว	2	ช้อนโต๊ะ
น้ำปลา	1 1/2	ช้อนโต๊ะ

วิธีทำ

1. ล้างกุ้งให้สะอาด แกะเปลือกออก เอาถุงมูลกุ้งบนหัวออก แล้วจึงนำไปย่างไฟให้พอสุก ๆ ดิบ ๆ นำกุ้งมาผ่าออกเป็นสองซีก จัดใส่จานที่รองด้วยผักกาดหอม
2. ผสมกระเทียม พริก น้ำปลา น้ำมะนาว ปรุงรสเผ็ด เปรี้ยว เค็ม ให้ได้รสจัดตามความต้องการ แล้วจึงนำไปราดบนตัวกุ้งที่เตรียมไว้ โรยผักชีเสิร์ฟ

Kung Sa

Spicy raw prawns

กุ้งซ่า

Ingredients

300 grams very fresh medium-sized white prawns
1/2 cup shredded cabbage
1 celery plant
20 hot chillies
50 garlic cloves
1/2 tsp. salt
3 tbsp. lime juice

Preparation

1. Wash, shell, and devein the prawns, leaving the tail fins in place, and arrange on a serving dish.
2. Chop the garlic and chillies together.
3. Mix the lime juice and salt so that a sour taste predominates over the salty ; then, add the chopped garlic and chilli.
4. When served, this sauce is spooned over the prawns, and they are eaten with the celery and cabbage.

เครื่องปรุง

กุ้งชีแฮ้สดขนาดกลาง	300	กรัม
กะหล่ำปลีหั่นฝอย	1/2	ถ้วย
ขึ้นฉ่าย	1	ต้น
พริกขี้หนูสด	20	เม็ด
กระเทียม	50	กลีบ
เกลือป่น	1/2	ช้อนชา
น้ำมะนาว	3	ช้อนโต๊ะ

วิธีทำ

1. ล้างกุ้งให้สะอาด แกะเปลือกออกเอาหางไว้ ผ่าหลังชักเส้นดำออก จัดวางเรียงบนจานเสิร์ฟ
2. สับกระเทียม พริกขี้หนูสดรวมกัน
3. ผสมน้ำมะนาว เกลือเข้าด้วยกันชิมรสให้มีรสเปรี้ยวนำเค็มตาม แล้วใส่กระเทียม พริกขี้หนูสับ
4. เวลารับประทานตักน้ำจิ้มราดบนตัวกุ้ง มีกะหล่ำปลีหั่นฝอยและขึ้นฉ่ายเป็นเครื่องเคียง

Lap Kai

Savory chopped chicken salad

ลาบไก่

Ingredients

2 cups chopped chicken breast with skin
2 tbsp. sliced shallot
2 tbsp. chopped phak chi farang
1/4 cup mint leaves
2-3 tbsp. ground parched rice
1-2 tbsp. ground dried chillies
4 tbsp. lime juice
3 tbsp. fish sauce
fresh vegetables : cucumbers, Yard-long beans, Chinese cabbage, lettuce spring onion,

Preparation

1. Mix 2 tablespoonsful of the lime juice with the chopped chicken. Place the chicken in a dry wok over moderate heat and stir until the chicken is done. Turn off the heat.
2. Toss with the chicken the rest of the lime juice, the fish sauce, ground parched rice, ground chilli, shallot, phakchi farang, and mint. Taste and season additionally as desired.
3. Serve with fresh vegetables.

Note : If you like giblets, you can cut these up into small pieces and dry fry with the chicken breast meat.

เครื่องปรุง

อกไก่ติดหนังสับ	๒	ถ้วย
หอมแดงซอย	๒	ช้อนโต๊ะ
ผักชีฝรั่งหั่น	๒	ช้อนโต๊ะ
สะระแหน่เด็ดเป็นใบ	๑/๔	ถ้วย
ข้าวคั่วป่น	๒-๓	ช้อนโต๊ะ
พริกป่น	๑-๒	ช้อนโต๊ะ
น้ำมะนาว	๔	ช้อนโต๊ะ
น้ำปลา	๓	ช้อนโต๊ะ

ผักสด แตงกวา ถั่วฝักยาว ผักกาดขาว ผักกาดหอม ต้นหอม

วิธีทำ

1. เนื้อไก่ผสมน้ำมะนาว 2 ช้อนโต๊ะ ตั้งไฟรวนให้ไก่สุก ยกลง
2. ใส่น้ำมะนาวอีก 2 ช้อนโต๊ะ น้ำปลา ข้าวคั่ว พริกป่น หอมซอย ผักชีฝรั่ง ใบสะระแหน่ เคล้าให้เข้ากัน ชิมรสตามชอบ
3. รับประทานกับผักสด

หมายเหตุ ถ้าชอบเครื่องในไก่ ให้ต้มให้สุกแล้วหั่นชิ้นเล็ก ๆ ใส่เมื่อรวนไก่จนสุกแล้ว

Pla Kao Rat Phrik

Fried grouper with chilli sauce

ปลาเก๋าราดพริก

Ingredients

1 grouper weighing 500 grams
15 hot chillies
10 shallots
10 garlic cloves
1 tsp. chopped coriander root
1 tbsp. palm sugar
3 tbsp. tamarind juice
2 tbsp. fish sauce

Preparation

1. Scale, clean, and wash the fish, score the flesh on either side attractively, and allow to drain.
2. Heat the 2 cups of oil in a deep wok. When hot, fry the grouper over medium heat. Wait until the fish is golden brown on one side before turning it over to fry on the other ; in this way, it will not stick to the wok. When nicely done on both sides, remove from the oil, drain, and place on a serving dish.
3. Peel the shallots and garlic, chop finely together with the chillies and coriander root, and then stir fry, using the 2 tbsp. of oil, until fragrant.
4. Add the tamarind juice, fish sauce, and palm sugar, and then pour over the grouper and serve.

เครื่องปรุง

ปลาเก๋าน้ำหนัก ๕๐๐ กรัม	๑	ตัว
พริกขี้หนู	๑๕	เม็ด
หอมแดง	๑๐	หัว
กระเทียม	๑๐	กลีบ
รากผักชี	๑	ช้อนชา
น้ำตาลปีบ	๑	ช้อนโต๊ะ
น้ำมะขามเปียก	๓	ช้อนโต๊ะ
น้ำปลา	๒	ช้อนโต๊ะ

วิธีทำ

1. ขอดเกล็ดปลา ควักไส้ออก ล้างปลาให้สะอาด บั้งทั้งสองด้านทิ้งไว้ให้สะเด็ดน้ำ
2. ตั้งกระทะก้นลึกใส่น้ำมัน 2 ถ้วย ใช้ไฟกลาง พอน้ำมันร้อนนำปลาลงทอด เมื่อปลาเหลืองดีแล้วจึงพลิกอีกด้านหนึ่ง ปลาจึงจะไม่ติดกระทะ เมื่อเหลืองกรอบทั้งสองด้านตักขึ้นให้สะเด็ดน้ำมัน พักไว้ในจานที่เตรียมเสิร์ฟ
3. ปอกเปลือกหอมแดงและกระเทียม สับหอม กระเทียมรวมกับรากผักชี พริกขี้หนูให้ละเอียด นำไปผัดในน้ำมัน 2 ช้อนโต๊ะให้หอม
4. ปรุงรสด้วยน้ำมะขามเปียก น้ำปลา น้ำตาลปีบ ให้ได้สามรส (เค็ม เปรี้ยว หวาน) ราดบนปลาที่เตรียมไว้ แล้วเสิร์ฟทันที

Pla Ka-phong Khao Phao

Sea perch broiled in banana leaf

ปลากะพงขาวเผา

Ingredients

1 sea perch weighing about 500 grams
2 tbsp. crisp-fried shallot slices
1 tsp. ground pepper
2 tbsp. light soy sauce
1 tbsp. oyster sauce

Preparation

1. Scale and clean the fish, wash well, and place in a bowl.
2. Stir together the soy sauce, pepper, and oyster sauce, rub the fish with this mixture, allow to marinate for about 30 minutes, and then rub the fish with the fried shallot.
3. Wrap the perch in banana leaf and then in aluminum foil and then roast over a charcoal fire. When done, remove the fish from the wrappings, arrange attractively on a platter, and serve with vegetables and this sauce.
4. Sauce : in a pot, simmer 1/2 cup tamarind juice , 3 tbsp. palm sugar, and 1 1/2 tbsp. soy sauce until thickened , then, remove from the heat, transfer to a small bowl, and sprinkle with the sliced chillies and shallots.

เครื่องปรุง

ปลากะพงขาว น้ำหนัก 500 กรัม	๑ ตัว
หอมแดงเจียว	๒ ช้อนโต๊ะ
พริกไทยป่น	๑ ช้อนชา
ซีอิ๊วขาว	๒ ช้อนโต๊ะ
น้ำมันหอย	๑ ช้อนโต๊ะ

วิธีทำ

1. ขอดเกล็ดปลากะพง ควักไส้ออก ล้างให้สะอาด ใส่ชาม พักไว้
2. ผสมซีอิ๊วขาวกับพริกไทย และน้ำมันหอย คนให้เข้ากัน เคล้ากับตัวปลา หมักประมาณ 30 นาที จึงคลุกปลากับหอมซอยทอด
3. ห่อปลากะพงด้วยใบตอง แล้วนำอะลูมินั่มฟอยล์ห่อชั้นนอกอีกที นำไปเผาไฟจนสุกดี แล้วแกะออกจากใบตอง จัดใส่จานให้สวยแต่งด้วยผักรับประทานกับน้ำจิ้ม
4. น้ำจิ้ม ให้ผสมน้ำมะขามเปียก 1/2 ถ้วย น้ำตาลปีบ 3 ช้อนโต๊ะ ซีอิ๊วขาว 1 1/2 ช้อนโต๊ะ ใส่หม้อตั้งไฟเคี่ยวให้จนเหนียว ยกลงจากเตา เทใส่ถ้วยน้ำจิ้ม โรยหน้าด้วยพริกขี้หนูซอย หอมซอย

Pla Chon Op Wai

Serpent-head baked with wine

ปลาช่อนอบไวน์

Ingredients

1 serpent-head fish weighing about 1 kilogram
1 tsp. ground pepper
2 tsp. salt
4 tbsp. white wine
1 tbsp. butter

Preparation

1. Scale the fish and wash thoroughly. Cut along the back from head to tail and open the body out. With a sharp knife, remove the bones. Remove the entrails, and wash well once again.
2. Rub the entire body with the salt and pepper and then apply the butter. Bake at 350 ° F. for about 25 minutes until golden ; then, pour the wine over the fish and bake for 5 more minutes. Serve with sauce and vegetable as you like.
3. Sauce : pound 10 garlic colves, 2 coriander roots, and 7 hot chillies until finely ground, transfer to small bowl, add 1 1/2 tbsp. lime juice and 1/2 tsp. salt, stir to mix, and serve with the serpent-head.

เครื่องปรุง

ปลาช่อน น้ำหนักประมาณ ๑ กิโลกรัม	๑ ตัว
พริกไทยป่น	๑ ช้อนชา
เกลือป่น	๒ ช้อนชา
ไวน์ขาว	๔ ช้อนโต๊ะ
เนย	๑ ช้อนโต๊ะ

วิธีทำ

1. ขอดเกล็ดปลาช่อนทั้งตัว ล้างให้สะอาด ผ่าหลังจากหัวลงมาถึงหางแบะออก ใช้มีดคมแซะกระดูกก้างกลางออก ควักไส้ทิ้ง ล้างให้สะอาดอีกครั้ง
2. ทาเกลือป่น พริกไทย ให้ทั่วตัวปลา แล้วทาเนย นำเข้าอบไฟ 350° ฟ. ประมาณ 25 นาที พอสุกเหลือง นำออกมาราดไวน์ขาวจนทั่วตัวแล้วนำเข้าอบต่ออีก 5 นาที เสิร์ฟกับน้ำจิ้มและผักสดตามชอบ
3. น้ำจิ้ม โขลกกระเทียม 10 กลีบ รากผักชี 2 ราก พริกขี้หนูสด 7 เม็ด จนละเอียด แล้วใส่ถ้วย เติมน้ำมะนาว 1 1/2 ช้อนโต๊ะ เกลือป่น 1/2 ช้อนชา คนให้เข้ากัน เสิร์ฟกับปลาช่อนอบ

Khai Luk Khoei

Fried hard-boiled eggs with tamarind sauce

ไข่ลูกเขย

Ingredients

10 unshelled boiled eggs (or duck eggs)
1/2 cup coriander leaves
7 crisp-fried dried hot chillies
3 tbsp. crisp fried shallot slices
1/3 cup palm sugar
1/2 cup tamarind juice
2 tbsp. fish sauce
1/4 cup cooking oil for frying

Preparation

1. Heat the oil in a wok. When hot, fry the eggs whole. When they are golden brown all over, remove and set aside.
2. In the 1 tablespoonful of oil used for frying the shallot, stir fry the palm sugar. Add the tamarind juice and fish sauce and continue stir frying until thickened. The taste should be sour, salty, and sweet. When ready, remove from the heat.
3. Before serving, cut the eggs in half and arrange on a plate with the yolks upward. Dip the sauce over the eggs and sprinkle them with the fried shallot, fried chillies, and coriander leaves.

เครื่องปรุง

ไข่เป็ดต้มสุกปอกเปลือก	10	ฟอง
ผักชีเด็ดเป็นใบ	1/2	ถ้วย
พริกขี้หนูแห้งทอด	7	เม็ด
หอมเจียว	3	ช้อนโต๊ะ
น้ำตาลปีบ	1/3	ถ้วย
น้ำมะขามเปียก	1/2	ถ้วย
น้ำปลา	2	ช้อนโต๊ะ
น้ำมัน	1	ถ้วย

วิธีทำ

1. ใส่น้ำมันในกระทะ ตั้งไฟพอร้อน เอาไข่ต้มลงทอดจนเหลืองทั่วฟอง ตักขึ้นพักไว้
2. ใส่น้ำตาลปีบลงผัดในน้ำมันเจียวหอม 1 ช้อนโต๊ะ ใส่น้ำมะขามเปียก น้ำปลา คนให้เข้ากัน เคี่ยวไปจนข้น ชิมรสให้เปรี้ยว เค็ม หวาน ปิดไฟ ยกลง
3. จัดเสิร์ฟโดยผ่าไข่ออกเป็นสองซีก วางหงายขึ้นบนจาน ราดด้วยน้ำมะขามเปียก โรยหอมเจียวและผักชี รับประทานกับพริกขี้หนูแห้งทอด

Si-khrong Mu Thot

Fried spareribs marinated in pineapple juice

ซี่โครงหมูทอด

Ingredients

1 kilogram tender spareribs
1 tbsp. finely-pounded garlic
1/2 tbsp. ground pepper
1 tbsp. ground roasted coriander seed
1 tbsp. brown sugar
1 tsp. salt
1/2 tbsp. dark soy sauce
1 tbsp. light soy sauce
1 tbsp. fish sauce
1/2 cup pineapple juice
cooking oil for frying

Preparation

1. Wash the spareribs, cut into bite-size pieces, and marinate in the pineapple juice for about half an hour.
2. Now, rub the ribs with a mixture of the dark soy sauce, light soy sauce, fish sauce, garlic, pepper, salt, sugar, and ground coriander seed and marinate for another half an hour or so.
3. Pour enough oil into a wok on medium heat to form a pool about an inch deep in the middle and fry the spareribs, a few pieces at a time, until mouth-wateringly golden brown. Remove from the oil and serve them with lettuce, pineapple, and spring onion.

เครื่องปรุง

ซี่โครงหมูอ่อน	1	กิโลกรัม
กระเทียมโขลกละเอียด	1	ช้อนโต๊ะ
พริกไทยป่น	1/2	ช้อนโต๊ะ
ลูกผักชีคั่วป่น	1	ช้อนโต๊ะ
น้ำตาลสีรำ	1	ช้อนโต๊ะ
เกลือป่น	1	ช้อนชา
ซีอิ๊วดำ	1/2	ช้อนโต๊ะ
ซีอิ๊วขาว	1	ช้อนโต๊ะ
น้ำปลา	1	ช้อนโต๊ะ
น้ำสับปะรดคั้น	1/2	ถ้วย
น้ำมันสำหรับทอด		

วิธีทำ

1. ล้างซี่โครงหมู สับเป็นท่อนสั้น ๆ หมักไว้กับน้ำสับปะรดประมาณ 30 นาที
2. คลุกซี่โครงหมูด้วยซีอิ๊วดำ ซีอิ๊วขาว น้ำปลา กระเทียม พริกไทย เกลือ น้ำตาลสีรำ และลูกผักชี หมักไว้ประมาณ 30 นาที
3. ทอดซี่โครงหมู ไฟปานกลางให้น้ำมันท่วมซี่โครงหมู พลิกหมูไปมาจนเหลือง เสิร์ฟกับผักกาดหอม สับปะรด และต้นหอม

Pla Kon

Fried fish cakes

ปลาก้อน

Ingredients

1 cup mashed steamed sole meat
3 tbsp. mashed boiled potato
1 tbsp. finely chopped celery or Chinese soup celery
5 green beans, boiled and cut into short lengths
1/2 carrot, boiled and sliced
1 egg
1/4 cup toasted bread crumbs
1/2 tsp. salt
2 tbsp. fresh milk
2 cups cooking oil for frying
absorbent paper

Preparation

1. Blend together the fish, potato, salt, celery, and egg, add the milk, and knead to mix.
2. Divide into five portions, mold each into a cake, and coat with the toasted bread crumbs. Deep fry in hot oil until golden brown.
3. Remove from the oil, drain on absorbent paper, and serve with the carrot and beans.

เครื่องปรุง

เนื้อปลาตาเดียวนึ่งสุก	1 ถ้วย
มันฝรั่งต้มบดละเอียด	3 ช้อนโต๊ะ
ขึ้นฉ่ายสับละเอียด	1 ช้อนโต๊ะ
ถั่วแขกหั่นท่อนสั้นต้ม	5 ฝัก
แครอทหั่นต้ม	1/2 หัว
ไข่	1 ฟอง
ผงขนมปังป่น	1/4 ถ้วย
เกลือป่น	1/2 ช้อนชา
นมสด	2 ช้อนโต๊ะ
น้ำมันสำหรับทอด	2 ถ้วย
กระดาษซับน้ำมัน	

วิธีทำ

1. ผสมปลา มันฝรั่ง เกลือ ขึ้นฉ่าย ไข่ เข้าด้วยกัน นวดเบา ๆ แล้วใส่นมสด นวดให้เข้ากัน
2. แบ่งส่วนผสมออกเป็น 5 ส่วน ปั้นเป็นก้อนรี ๆ คลุกผงขนมปังป่นให้ทั่ว ทอดในน้ำมันร้อน ๆ ไฟกลาง ทอดให้เป็นสีเหลืองทอง
3. ตักออกวางบนกระดาษซับน้ำมัน เสิร์ฟกับถั่วแขกต้ม และแครอทต้ม

Kung Kra-thiam Phrik Thai

Fried prawns in pepper and garlic

กุ้งกระเทียมพริกไทย

Ingredients

500 grams fresh prawns
1 tsp. finely sliced spring onion
2 spring onions
2 tbsp. crushed garlic
1 tsp. ground pepper
1 tsp. salt
1 tbsp. lime juice
1/4 cup butter

Preparation

1. Wash and shell the prawns, leaving the tail fins on, and slit down the back and remove the dark vein.
2. Heat the butter in a wok and sauté the garlic until fragrant ; then, add the prawns, 1/2 teaspoonful of the pepper, the salt, and the lime juice, stir fry, and when the prawns are done, remove from the wok.
3. Sprinkle the prawns with sliced spring onion and pepper, and serve with the spring onions.

เครื่องปรุง

กุ้งสด	๕๐๐ กรัม
ต้นหอมซอย	๑ ช้อนชา
ต้นหอม	๒ ต้น
กระเทียมทุบ	๒ ช้อนโต๊ะ
พริกไทยป่น	๑ ช้อนชา
เกลือป่น	๑ ช้อนชา
น้ำมะนาว	๑ ช้อนโต๊ะ
เนยสด	๑/๔ ถ้วย

วิธีทำ

1. ล้างกุ้ง ปอกเปลือกไว้หาง ผ่าหลังชักเส้นดำออก
2. ใส่เนยสดลงในกระทะ ใส่กระเทียม เจียวให้หอม ใส่กุ้ง พริกไทย 1/2 ช้อนชา เกลือ น้ำมะนาว พอกุ้งสุก ตักขึ้น
3. โรยพริกไทย ต้นหอมซอย รับประทานกับต้นหอม

Pla Meuk Thot

Fried squid

ปลาหมึกทอด

Ingredients

500 grams medium-sized squid
150 grams tapioca flour
1 tsp. ground pepper
1 1/2 tbsp. light soy sauce
50 grams garlic
2 cups cooking oil for frying

Preparation

1. Wash the squid, remove the inedible parts, and cut crosswise into slices 1 inch wide.
2. Pound the garlic and pepper until finely ground. Mix this thoroughly with the squid, add the soy sauce, and then allow to stand for a short while.
3. Mix the squid with the tapioca flour and fry in medium-hot oil. When browned, transfer to a dish and serve with chilli sauce.

เครื่องปรุง

ปลาหมึกกล้วย		
ขนาดกลาง	500	กรัม
แป้งมัน	150	กรัม
พริกไทยป่น	1	ช้อนชา
ซีอิ๊วขาว	1 1/2	ช้อนโต๊ะ
กระเทียม	50	กรัม
น้ำมันสำหรับทอด	2	ถ้วย

วิธีทำ

1. ล้างปลาหมึกให้สะอาด เอาส่วนที่รับประทานไม่ได้ออก หั่นตามขวางเป็นชิ้นขนาด 1 นิ้ว
2. โขลกกระเทียมกับพริกไทยให้ละเอียด นำมาเคล้ากับปลาหมึก ใส่ซีอิ๊วขาว หมักไว้สักครู่
3. เคล้าปลาหมึกกับแป้งมัน ทอดในน้ำมันร้อนปานกลาง จนปลาหมึกสุกเหลือง ตักใส่จานรับประทานกับซอสพริก

Neua Daet Diao

Fried sun-dried beef

เนื้อแดดเดียว

Ingredients

500 grams beef
1 garlic bulb
3 coriander roots
1 tsp. curry powder
1/2 tsp. ground pepper
1 tbsp. sugar
2 tbsp. whiskey
2 tbsp. oyster sauce
2 tbsp. fish sauce
3-4 cups cooking oil for deep frying

Preparation

1. Wash the beef well and cut into strips about 1 cm. thick.
2. Pound the garlic, coriander roots, and pepper together until finely ground. Rub this into the beef, add the fish sauce, whiskey, oyster sauce, sugar, and curry powder, work around together, and then allow to marinate for about an hour. Then, lay the strips out in the sun and leave them for one day, turning from time to time.
3. Deep fry the beef in hot oil. When done, drain and serve with chilli sauce, lettuce, sliced tomato and cucumber.

เครื่องปรุง

เนื้อวัว	500	กรัม
กระเทียม	1	หัว
รากผักชี	3	ราก
ผงกะหรี่	1	ช้อนชา
พริกไทยป่น	1/2	ช้อนชา
น้ำตาลทราย	1	ช้อนโต๊ะ
วิสกี้	2	ช้อนโต๊ะ
น้ำมันหอย	2	ช้อนโต๊ะ
น้ำปลา	2	ช้อนโต๊ะ
น้ำมันสำหรับทอด	3-4	ถ้วย

วิธีทำ

1. ล้างเนื้อให้สะอาด แล่ออกเป็นแผ่นบางขนาด 1 ซม.
2. โขลกกระเทียม รากผักชี พริกไทยให้ละเอียด นำเนื้อลงเคล้า เติมน้ำปลา วิสกี้ น้ำมันหอย น้ำตาลทราย ผงกะหรี่ หมักไว้ประมาณ 1 ชั่วโมง แล้วตากแดด 1 วัน
3. ทอดเนื้อในน้ำมันร้อน พอสุกตักขึ้นให้สะเด็ดน้ำมัน เสิร์ฟกับซอสพริก ผักกาดหอม มะเขือเทศและแตงกวา

Pla Thot Kleua

Fried fish steaks

ปลาทอดเกลือ

Ingredients

1 or 2 sea perch or Spanish mackerel steaks
1 tsp. salt
2 slices of lime
cooking oil for frying

Preparation

1. Wash the steaks. Cut so they are about half the size of the palm of the hand. The pieces should not be too thick, for they would not become done all the way through. Rub the fish with the salt.
2. Fry the fish over medium heat. When done and golden, remove from the oil, place on a dish, squeeze a little lime onto the fish, and serve.

เครื่องปรุง

ปลากะพง หรือ	
ปลาอินทรี	1-2 ชิ้น
เกลือป่น	1 ช้อนชา
มะนาวฝาน	2 ชิ้น
น้ำมันสำหรับทอด	

วิธีทำ

1. ล้างปลา แล่เป็นชิ้นขนาดครึ่งฝ่ามือ อย่าให้หนาเกินไป เพราะจะทำให้สุกยาก นำมาคลุกเกลือ
2. ทอดปลา ไฟขนาดกลาง ให้เหลืองพอสุก ตักออกจัดใส่จาน บีบมะนาวราดปลาเล็กน้อย เสิร์ฟ

Kung Thot Khem

Salty fried prawns

กุ้งทอดเค็ม

Ingredients

500 grams white prawns
1 tsp. salt
1 cup cooking oil for frying

Preparation

1. Wash the prawns and cut their feelers off ; they need not be shelled.
2. Place the prawns in a pot and rub them thoroughly with the salt and allow them to rest a few minutes. Pour the oil into a wok over medium heat, and when good and hot, fry the prawns. When they are done and golden brown, remove them from the oil and drain.
3. Place the prawns on a serving dish ; they will have a salty tang.

เครื่องปรุง

กุ้งชีแฮ้	๕๐๐	กรัม
เกลือป่น	๑	ช้อนชา
น้ำมันสำหรับทอด	๑	ถ้วย

วิธีทำ

1. สับหนวดกุ้งออก ล้างให้สะอาด ไม่ต้องปอกเปลือก
2. ใส่กุ้งลงในหม้อ ใส่เกลือ เคล้าให้เข้ากัน หมักทิ้งไว้สักครู่ ตั้งกระทะไฟกลาง พอน้ำมันร้อนจัด ใส่กุ้งลงทอดจนสุกเหลือง ตักขึ้นให้สะเด็ดน้ำมัน
3. ตักใส่จานเสิร์ฟ กุ้งจะมีรสเค็ม

Seua Rong Hai

Spicy broiled beef

เสือร้องไห้

Ingredients

300 grams beef with fat
1 tbsp. light soy sauce
1 tsp. fish sauce

Preparation

1. Wash the beef and then marinate with the soy and fish sauces for between one and two hours.
2. Broil the meat over a low charcoal fire until done to the desired degree, cut into thin slices, and serve with the sauce and spring onions.

Sauce Ingredients

1 tsp. ground dried chillies
1 tsp. ground parched rice
1 tbsp. thinly sliced shallot
2 tbsp. lime juice
3 tbsp. fish sauce

Mix the ingredients together and serve in small bowl.

เครื่องปรุง

เนื้อวัวส่วนอกมีมันติด 300	กรัม
ซีอิ๊วขาว	1 ช้อนโต๊ะ
น้ำปลา	1 ช้อนชา

วิธีทำ

1. ล้างเนื้อให้สะอาด เคล้ากับซีอิ๊วขาว น้ำปลา หมักไว้ 1-2 ชั่วโมง
2. ย่างเนื้อบนเตาถ่านไฟอ่อน พอสุกมีกลิ่นหอม หั่นชิ้นบาง ๆ รับประทานกับน้ำจิ้มและต้นหอม

เครื่องปรุงน้ำจิ้ม

พริกป่น	1 ช้อนชา
ข้าวคั่วป่น	1 ช้อนชา
หอมแดงซอย	1 ช้อนโต๊ะ
น้ำมะนาว	2 ช้อนโต๊ะ
น้ำปลา	3 ช้อนโต๊ะ

ผสมพริกป่น ข้าวคั่ว หอมแดงซอย น้ำมะนาว น้ำปลาเข้าด้วยกัน รับประทานกับเนื้อย่าง

Thot Man Neua Sap

Fried spiced meatballs

ทอดมันเนื้อสับ

Ingredients

300 grams ground beef
1-2 eggs, beaten
3 medium-sized potatoes
3 stalks Chinese celery, chopped fine
3 thin slices of nutmeg
1/2 cup wheat flour
15 peppercorns
1 1/2 tsp. salt
cooking oil for frying

Preparation

1. Boil the potatoes and then dice them.
2. Pound the pepper, nutmeg, and salt until finely ground, add to the ground beef and diced potatoes, and mix thoroughly. (Take a small amount, wrap it in banana leaf, roast, and taste ; if not salty enough, add salt.)
3. Mix the celery with the beef and potato, form into balls about the size of a small egg, smear with beaten egg, and flour.
4. Pour oil into a wok over high heat and fry the meatballs until crisp and golden brown on the outside.
5. Serve hot with catsup or chilli sauce.

เครื่องปรุง

เนื้อวัวบด	300	กรัม
ไข่ตีเข้ากัน	1-2	ฟอง
มันฝรั่งขนาดกลาง	3	หัว
ขึ้นฉ่ายหั่นละเอียด	3	ต้น
ลูกจันทน์เทศฝานบาง	3	แว่น
แป้งสาลี	1/2	ถ้วย
พริกไทยเม็ด	15	เม็ด
เกลือป่น	1 1/2	ช้อนชา
น้ำมันสำหรับทอด		

วิธีทำ

1. ต้มมันฝรั่งให้สุก หั่นเป็นชิ้นสี่เหลี่ยมเล็ก ๆ
2. โขลกพริกไทย ลูกจันทน์ เกลือ ให้ละเอียด ใส่เนื้อ มันฝรั่ง ลงเคล้า (ห่อใบตองปิ้งชิมรสดู ถ้าอ่อนเค็มเติมเกลือ)
3. ใส่ขึ้นฉ่ายลงผสม แล้วปั้นเป็นก้อน ๆ เท่าไข่ไก่ แล้วนำไปชุบไข่ให้ทั่วทั้งก้อน โรยด้วยแป้งสาลี
4. ใส่น้ำมันในกระทะ ใช้ไฟแรง ทอดเนื้อให้ข้างนอกเหลืองกรอบข้างในนุ่ม
5. เสิร์ฟร้อน ๆ พร้อมซอสพริก หรือซอสมะเขือเทศ

Mu Krop

Crisp-fried pork belly

หมูกรอบ

Ingredients

1 kilogram pork belly with thick lean layers
1 tbsp. salt
1/2 cup vinegar
1 tbsp. honey
cooking oil for frying

Preparation

1. Cut the pork lengthwise into four equal pieces and wash.
2. Boil the pork in water, add 2 teaspoonful of salt, boil about 30-40 minutes, remove from the water, and place on a gridiron.
3. In a pot , simmer the vinegar and the honey until melted. Spoon this sauce over the pork, continue this for awhile, and then sprinkle the pork on all sides with the salt. Next, hang the pork in a breezy spot or in the wind of an electric fan until dry.
4. With a fork, prick the skin and flesh on all surfaces of the pork. Deep fry until crisp and golden brown, drain, cut into bite-size slices, and serve.

เครื่องปรุง

หมูสามชั้น	1 กิโลกรัม
เกลือป่น	1 ช้อนโต๊ะ
น้ำส้มสายชู	1/2 ถ้วย
น้ำผึ้ง	1 ช้อนโต๊ะ
น้ำมันสำหรับทอด	

วิธีทำ

1. หมูสามชั้นล้างน้ำให้สะอาด หั่นตามยาวให้หนาประมาณ 1 นิ้ว
2. ต้มน้ำให้เดือด ใส่หมูสามชั้นลงต้ม ใส่เกลือ 2 ช้อนชา ต้มนาน 30-40 นาที เอาหมูขึ้นวางบนตะแกรงผึ่งไว้
3. เทน้ำส้มสายชูและน้ำผึ้งลงในหม้อ ตั้งไฟให้เดือด ตักราดบนหมูหลายครั้ง ใช้มือแตะเกลือทาบนชิ้นหมูให้ทั่ว แขวนหมูสามชั้นผึ่งลมไว้ให้แห้ง
4. ใช้ส้อมจิ้มหนังหมูให้ทั่วชิ้นหมู นำไปทอดในน้ำมันมาก จนกระทั่งหมูมีสีเหลือง กรอบ ตักขึ้นให้สะเด็ดน้ำมัน หั่นเป็นชิ้นพอคำ เสิร์ฟ

Pla Samli Chup Paeng Thot

Kingfish fried in batter

ปลาสำลีชุบแป้งทอด

Ingredients

1 kingfish
1/2 cup wheat flour
1/4 cup water
cooking oil for frying

Preparation

1. Clean the fish, wash well, slice open down the length of the back, and remove the bones.
2. Mix the flour and water.
3. Heat enough oil to deep fry the fish in a wok. Dip the fish into the batter so that it is coated completely. Fry the fish until golden brown, transfer to a plate, and serve with chilli sauce or some other sauce you like.

เครื่องปรุง

ปลาสำลี	1	ตัว
แป้งสาลี	1/2	ถ้วย
น้ำ	1/4	ถ้วย
น้ำมันสำหรับทอด		

วิธีทำ

1. ควักไส้ปลาออก ล้างให้สะอาด ผ่ากลาง เลาะก้างปลาออก
2. ผสมแป้งกับน้ำ
3. ใส่น้ำมันสำหรับทอดในกระทะ กะน้ำมันให้ท่วมตัวปลา ตั้งไฟ เอาปลาชุบแป้งให้ทั่ว ทอดให้เหลือง ตักใส่จาน เสิร์ฟกับซอสพริก หรือน้ำจิ้มตามชอบ

Pla Insi Thot

Fried spanish mackerel steak

ปลาอินทรีทอด

Ingredients

1 Spanish mackerel steak weighing 200 grams
1 tsp. salt
cooking oil for frying

Preparation

1. Wash the mackerel steak. Dissolve the salt in enough water to cover the steak and soak it for about 10 minutes. Rinse the steak once in fresh water and then allow to dry.
2. Fry the mackerel steak in medium-hot oil until golden brown, remove from the oil, drain, place on a dish, and serve.

Note : Chilli fish sauce (See page 5)

เครื่องปรุง

เนื้อปลาอินทรี น้ำหนัก 200 กรัม	1 ชิ้น
เกลือป่น	1 ช้อนชา
น้ำมันสำหรับทอด	

วิธีทำ

1. ล้างปลาอินทรี แล้วแช่ในน้ำเกลือ (ผสมเกลือกับน้ำพอท่วมปลา) ประมาณ 10 นาที เอาขึ้นล้างน้ำออก 1 ครั้ง แล้วผึ่งให้แห้ง
2. ทอดปลาในน้ำมันร้อนปานกลางจนออกสีเหลือง ตักขึ้นให้สะเด็ดน้ำมัน จัดวางลงจานเสิร์ฟกับน้ำปลาพริกมะนาว

หมายเหตุ ดูคำอธิบายน้ำปลาพริกมะนาวในบทนำ

Pla Jalamet Khao Thot

Fried pomfret

ปลาจะละเม็ดขาวทอด

Ingredients

1 white pomfret weighing between 500 and 600 grams
1 tbsp. tapioca flour
3 cups cooking oil for frying

Preparation

1. Wash and clean the pomfret, score the flesh on both sides, and flour it with the tapioca flour.
2. Pour the oil into a wok on medium heat, and when it is hot, fry the pomfret golden brown on both sides ; then, remove from the oil, drain, and serve with the sauce and fresh vegetables.

Sauce Ingredients

3-4 hot chillies, sliced thin
1-2 shallots, sliced thin
1 tbsp. lime juice
1 tbsp. fish sauce

Mix all the ingredients together and serve in a small bowl.

เครื่องปรุง

ปลาจะละเม็ดขาว น้ำหนัก 500-600 กรัม	1 ตัว
แป้งมัน	1 ช้อนโต๊ะ
น้ำมันสำหรับทอด	3 ถ้วย

วิธีทำ

1. ล้างปลาจะละเม็ดให้สะอาด ควักไส้ออก บั้งตัวปลาทั้งสองข้าง แล้วนำปลามาคลุกกับแป้งมัน
2. ใส่น้ำมันลงในกระทะ ใช้ไฟกลาง พอน้ำมันร้อนใส่ปลาลงทอดสุกเหลือง ตักขึ้นให้สะเด็ดน้ำมัน รับประทานกับน้ำจิ้ม และผักสด

เครื่องปรุงน้ำจิ้ม

พริกขี้หนูซอย	3-4 เม็ด
หอมแดงซอย	1-2 หัว
น้ำมะนาว	1 ช้อนโต๊ะ
น้ำปลา	1 ช้อนโต๊ะ

ผสมหอมซอย พริกขี้หนูซอย น้ำปลา น้ำมะนาวเข้าด้วยกัน

Pla Ma-nao

Fried buttered Spanish mackerel steaks

ปลามะนาว

Ingredients

2 Spanish mackerel steaks
1/4 cup wheat flour
1/4 tsp. ground dried chillies
1/4 tsp. ground pepper
1/2 tsp. salt
2 tsp. lime juice
a quarter of a 227g bar of butter, melted
cooking oil for frying

Preparation

1. Mix the melted butter and lime juice in a bowl and set aside.
2. In another bowl, mix the flour, salt, and pepper.
3. Dip the fish in the butter and then coat with the flour.
4. Deep fry the fish. When done, place on a dish, sprinkle with a little ground dried chilli, and serve.

เครื่องปรุง

ปลาอินทรีหั่นตามขวาง	๒	ชิ้น
แป้งสาลี	๑/๔	ถ้วย
พริกป่น	๑/๔	ช้อนชา
พริกไทยป่น	๑/๔	ช้อนชา
เกลือป่น	๑/๒	ช้อนชา
น้ำมะนาว	๒	ช้อนชา
เนยละลาย	๑/๔	ก้อน
น้ำมันสำหรับทอด		

วิธีทำ

1. ผสมเนยละลายและน้ำมะนาวในชาม พักไว้
2. ผสมแป้งสาลี เกลือ พริกไทย ในอีกชามหนึ่ง
3. นำเนื้อปลาลงจุ่มในเนยละลายที่ผสมไว้ แล้วคลุกปลาในแป้งที่เตรียมไว้
4. ใส่น้ำมันในกระทะ ใส่ปลาทอดให้สุก ตักใส่จาน โรยพริกป่นเล็กน้อย แล้วเสิร์ฟ

Pla Darp Thot

Fried dorab

ปลาดาบทอด

Ingredients

1 dorab
2 tsp. salt
1 cup cooking oil for frying

Preparation

1. Wash and clean the fish, and then cut it into four pieces.
2. Rub the fish with the salt, allow to rest for a short time, and then wash in fresh water.
3. Pour the oil into a wok on high heat. When the oil is very hot, fry the fish so that it is crisp on the outside and tender inside.
4. Serve as is or with light soy sauce or chilli fish sauce some other sauce you like.

Note : Chilli fish sauce (See page 5)

เครื่องปรุง

ปลาดาบยาว	๑ ตัว
เกลือป่น	๒ ช้อนชา
น้ำมันสำหรับทอด	๑ ถ้วย

วิธีทำ

1. ล้างปลาให้สะอาด ควักไส้ทิ้ง หั่นเป็นสี่ชิ้น
2. ซาวปลากับเกลือ ทิ้งไว้สักครู่ แล้วล้างน้ำ
3. ใส่น้ำมันลงในกระทะ ตั้งไฟให้ร้อน ใช้ไฟแรง พอน้ำมันร้อนจัด ใส่ปลาลงทอด ให้ข้างนอกกรอบ ข้างในนุ่ม
4. จะรับประทานเลย หรือจิ้มกับซีอิ๊วขาว หรือจิ้มกับน้ำปลาพริกมะนาว

หมายเหตุ ดูคำอธิบายน้ำปลาพริกมะนาวในบทนำ

Pla Thu Priao Wan

Fried mackerel in sweet and sour sauce

ปลาทูเปรี้ยวหวาน

Ingredients

2 fresh short-bodied mackerel
1 coriander plant
4 red spur chillies
7 garlic cloves
2 tbsp. sugar
2 tbsp. tamarind juice
2 tbsp. fish sauce
1/2 cup water
5 tbsp. cooking oil

Preparation

1. Wash and clean the mackerel
2. Heat 3 tablespoonful of the oil in a wok. When it is hot, fry the fish golden brown, remove, and set aside.
3. Pound the chillies and garlic well.
4. Heat 2 tablespoonful of the oil in a wok. When hot, stir fry the pounded garlic and chilli until fragrant, add the tamarind juice, fish sauce, and sugar, and mix.
5. Return the fried mackerel to the wok, add the water, simmer to allow the sauce to penetrate the fish, taste and season additionally as desired, and then turn off the heat.
6. Garnish with coriander greens before serving.

เครื่องปรุง

ปลาทูสด	๒ ตัว
ผักชี	๑ ต้น
พริกชี้ฟ้าแดง	๔ เม็ด
กระเทียม	๗ กลีบ
น้ำตาลทราย	๒ ช้อนโต๊ะ
น้ำมะขามเปียก	๒ ช้อนโต๊ะ
น้ำปลา	๒ ช้อนโต๊ะ
น้ำ	๑/๒ ถ้วย
น้ำมัน	๕ ช้อนโต๊ะ

วิธีทำ

1. ล้างปลาทูให้สะอาด ควักไส้ออก
2. ใส่น้ำมัน 3 ช้อนโต๊ะในกระทะ ตั้งไฟให้ร้อน นำปลาทูลงทอดให้เหลือง ใส่จานไว้
3. โขลกพริกกับกระเทียม
4. ใส่น้ำมัน 2 ช้อนโต๊ะในกระทะ พอร้อน ใส่เครื่องที่โขลก ผัดให้หอม ใส่น้ำมะขามเปียก น้ำปลา น้ำตาลทราย ผัดให้เข้ากัน
5. ใส่ปลาทูที่เตรียมไว้ ใส่น้ำ ต้มไปจนเครื่องเข้าเนื้อปลาทู ชิมรสตามชอบ ปิดไฟ
6. เวลาเสิร์ฟแต่งหน้าด้วยผักชี

Tom Yam Kung

Sour and spicy prawn soup

ต้มยำกุ้ง

Ingredients

6 large spiny-clawed prawns
1 lemon grass stem, cut into short lengths
2-3 kaffir lime leaves, torn into pieces
5-6 crushed hot chillies
3 tbsp. lime juice
1-2 tbsp. fish sauce
3 cups soup stock

Preparation

1. Shell and devein the prawns and remove all inedible parts.
2. Heat the stock in a pot. When it is boiling, put in the lemon grass and then the prawns. Season with the fish sauce, chillies, and lime juice. Then, add the kaffir lime leaves remove from the heat, and serve hot.

Note : Ground dried chillies can be substituted for the hot chillies in this recipe ; add 1 teaspoonful of ground dried chillies to the boiling stock.

เครื่องปรุง

กุ้งนางตัวใหญ่	๖	ตัว
ตะไคร้หั่นเป็นท่อนสั้น ๆ	๑	ต้น
ใบมะกรูดฉีกหยาบ ๆ	๒-๓	ใบ
พริกขี้หนูบุบพอแตก	๕-๖	เม็ด
น้ำมะนาว	๓	ช้อนโต๊ะ
น้ำปลา	๑-๒	ช้อนโต๊ะ
น้ำซุป	๓	ถ้วย

วิธีทำ

1. แกะเปลือกกุ้ง ชักเส้นดำออก ดึงส่วนที่กินไม่ได้ออก ใช้ทั้งตัว
2. ใส่น้ำซุปลงในหม้อตั้งไฟ พอเดือดใส่ตะไคร้ ใส่กุ้ง ปรุงรสด้วยน้ำปลา พริกขี้หนู น้ำมะนาว ใส่ใบมะกรูด ยกลงเสิร์ฟร้อน ๆ

หมายเหตุ ใช้พริกป่นแทนพริกขี้หนูก็ได้ โดยใช้พริกป่น 1 ช้อนชา ละลายในหม้อน้ำซุป

Tom Kha Kai

Chicken boiled with galangal in coconut milk

ต้มข่าไก่

Ingredients

300 grams chicken meat
1/2 cup thin slices of young galangal
1 lemon grass stem, cut into slices
5 kaffir lime leaves, torn into pieces
5-6 small hot chillies, broken open
5 shallots, crushed
1 cup coconut cream
2 1/2 cups coconut milk
1 tbsp. salt
3 tbsp. lime juice
2 tbsp. fish sauce

Preparation

1. Wash the chicken and cut it into thin slices.
2. Bring the coconut milk to a boil and add the galangal, lemon grass, shallot, and kaffir lime leaves. Add the chicken, salt and simmer slowly over low heat. When the chicken is done, pour the coconut cream onto the soup, stir gently, and when the soup returns to a boil, turn off the heat.
3. Add the fish sauce, lime juice, and chillies, transfer to a bowl, and serve hot.

เครื่องปรุง

เนื้อไก่	300	กรัม
ข่าอ่อนหั่นบาง ๆ	1/2	ถ้วย
ตะไคร้	1	ต้น
ใบมะกรูดฉีก	5	ใบ
พริกขี้หนูสวนทุบ	5-6	เม็ด
หอมแดงทุบ	5	หัว
หัวกะทิ	1	ถ้วย
หางกะทิ	2 1/2	ถ้วย
เกลือป่น	1	ช้อนโต๊ะ
น้ำมะนาว	3	ช้อนโต๊ะ
น้ำปลา	2	ช้อนโต๊ะ

วิธีทำ

1. ล้างเนื้อไก่ หั่นชิ้นบาง
2. ใส่หางกะทิลงในหม้อ ตั้งไฟให้เดือด ใส่ข่าอ่อน ตะไคร้หั่นท่อนสั้น หอมแดง ใบมะกรูด ใส่เนื้อไก่ เกลือ เคี่ยวไฟอ่อน พอไก่สุก ราดหัวกะทิคนเบา ๆ เดือดอีกครั้ง ปิดไฟ
3. ใส่น้ำปลา น้ำมะนาว พริกขี้หนู ตักใส่ชาม รับประทานร้อน ๆ

Tom Yam Het

Sour and spicy mushroom soup

ต้มยำเห็ด

Ingredients

500 grams rice-straw mushrooms
2 lemon grass stems
4-5 kaffir lime leaves
10 hot chillies
2-3 dried chillies
1 coriander plant
1/2 tsp. salt
2-3 tbsp. fish sauce
2-3 tbsp. lime juice

Preparation

1. Wash the mushrooms, and cut into pieces.
2. Cut the lemon grass into lengths and crush them. Tear the kaffir lime leaves. Pick the leaves from the coriander plant. Hit the hot chillies with a pestle just enough to break them open. Roast the dried chillies and then tear them into pieces.
3. Heat 4 cups water in a pot. When it boils, put in the lemon grass, kaffir lime leaves, and mushrooms. Season with fish sauce and salt. When the mushrooms are done, take the pot off the heat and add the lime juice and both kinds of chillies.
4. Dip the soup into a serving dish and sprinkle with coriander leaves.

เครื่องปรุง

เห็ดสด เห็ดฟาง	500 กรัม
ตะไคร้	2 ต้น
ใบมะกรูดฉีก	4-5 ใบ
พริกขี้หนู	10 เม็ด
พริกขี้หนูแห้ง	2-3 เม็ด
ผักชี	1 ต้น
เกลือป่น	1/2 ช้อนชา
น้ำปลา	2-3 ช้อนโต๊ะ
น้ำมะนาว	2-3 ช้อนโต๊ะ

วิธีทำ

1. ล้างเห็ดเอาดินออก หั่นเป็นชิ้น ๆ
2. ตะไคร้หั่นเป็นท่อน ๆ ทุบ ใบมะกรูดฉีก ผักชีเด็ดเป็นใบ ๆ พริกขี้หนูบุบพอแตก พริกแห้งเผาฉีกเป็นชิ้น ๆ
3. ใส่น้ำมันลงในหม้อ 4 ถ้วย ตั้งไฟ พอเดือดใส่ตะไคร้ ใบมะกรูด เห็ด ปรุงรสด้วยน้ำปลา เกลือ พอเห็ดสุกยกลง ใส่พริกขี้หนู พริกขี้หนู-แห้ง น้ำมะนาว
4. ตักใส่ชามโรยด้วยผักชี

Tom Yam Kha Mu

Sour and spicy fresh pork hock soup

ต้มยำขาหมู

Ingredients

1 kilogram fresh pork hock
3 lemon grass stems
6 kaffir lime leaves
6 roasted dried spur chillies
2 tbsp. lime juice
3 tbsp. fish sauce
5 cups water

Preparation

1. Singe the hock over a fire until the skin turns yellow. Scrape with a knife to remove any hair. Wash, and then cut into disk-shaped slices.
2. Pour the water into a pot. Crush the lemon grass, slice into short lengths, and add to the pot. Tear the kaffir lime leaves into pieces and add to the pot. Put in the pork and place the pot over low heat. When the water boils, skim off the fat floating on the surface, simmer slowly until the pork is tender, and then remove from the heat. Be careful not to overcook.
3. Place lime juice and fish sauce in a bowl with torn spur chilli, dip the hot soup into the bowl, stir gently, taste and season additionally as you like, and then serve right away.

เครื่องปรุง

ขาหมู (เลือกซื้อขาหน้า)	๑ กิโลกรัม
ตะไคร้	๓ ต้น
ใบมะกรูด	๖ ใบ
พริกชี้ฟ้าแห้งเผา	๖ เม็ด
น้ำมะนาว	๒ ช้อนโต๊ะ
น้ำปลา	๓ ช้อนโต๊ะ
น้ำ	๕ ถ้วย

วิธีทำ

1. เอาขาหมูไปเผาไฟจนเหลืองทั่ว ใช้มีดขูดขนออกให้หมด ล้างน้ำให้สะอาด ตัดเป็นแว่น ๆ
2. ใส่น้ำลงในหม้อ ใส่ตะไคร้ทุบตัดท่อนสั้น ใบมะกรูดฉีก ใส่ขาหมู ยกขึ้นตั้งไฟ ใช้ไฟอ่อน พอเดือดช้อนน้ำมันที่ลอยทิ้ง เคี่ยวไฟรุม ๆ จนหนังหมูเปื่อย แต่อย่าให้เนื้อหมูเละ ยกลง
3. จัดเสิร์ฟโดยตักน้ำมะนาว น้ำปลา ฉีกพริกชี้ฟ้าแห้งใส่ถ้วย ตักขาหมูต้มร้อน ๆ ใส่ คนเบา ๆ ชิมรสตามชอบ เสิร์ฟทันที

Tun Ma-ra Yat Sai

Boiled stuffed bitter gourd

ตุ๋นมะระยัดไส้

Ingredients

2 Chinese bitter gourds
200 grams white prawns
200 grams pork
1 1/2 tbsp. fish sauce
1 1/2 cups soup stock or water

Preparation

1. Wash the bitter gourds, cut them crosswise into 3-inch sections, and remove the insides with a fork.
2. Wash the prawns and shell them ; only the meat is used.
3. Chop the prawn and pork together, mix in the fish sauce, and fill the bitter gourd sections with the mixture.
4. Place the filled sections in a pot, pour in the stock, put the lid on the pot, and simmer until the gourd is tender. Taste, and add more fish sauce if you wish.

เครื่องปรุง

มะระจีน	๒ ลูก
กุ้งชีแฮ้	๒๐๐ กรัม
เนื้อหมู	๒๐๐ กรัม
น้ำปลา	๑ ๑/๒ ช้อนโต๊ะ
น้ำซุปหรือน้ำ	๑ ๑/๒ ถ้วย

วิธีทำ

1. ล้างมะระ หั่นตามขวางเป็นท่อน 3 นิ้ว ใช้ส้อมควักไส้มะระออก
2. ล้างกุ้งให้สะอาด ปอกเปลือกออก เอาแต่เนื้อ
3. สับกุ้งกับเนื้อหมู แล้วเคล้ากับน้ำปลา นำไปใส่เป็นไส้มะระ
4. เรียงมะระลงในถ้วยตุ๋น ใส่น้ำซุป นำไปตุ๋นจนมะระสุกนุ่ม ชิมรส ถ้าอ่อนเค็มเติมน้ำปลาได้

Kaeng Jeut Khai Jiao

Omelette in broth

แกงจืดไข่เจียว

Ingredients

3-4 eggs
1-2 lettuce plants
1 tsp. dried salted vegetable
1 coriander plant
1 tsp. chopped garlic
1/2 tsp. ground pepper
2-3 tbsp. fish sauce
5 cups soup stock or water
4 tbsp. cooking oil

Preparation

1. Bring the stock to a boil. If you wish to add pork, drop small lumps of the ground meat into the stock.
2. Beat the eggs and fry in a wok until firm. Now, move the egg off to one side, put in the garlic, and saute until fragrant and golden. Next, return the egg to the middle, break up with the spatula into pieces, transfer the contents of the wok to the pot, and when the stock returns to a boil, add the fish sauce.
3. Place lettuce leaves in a bowl, dip the soup into the bowl, sprinkle with the pepper, coriander greens, and dried salted vegetable, and serve hot.

เครื่องปรุง

ไข่	3-4 ฟอง
ผักกาดหอม	1-2 ต้น
ตังฉ่าย	1 ช้อนชา
ผักชี	1 ต้น
กระเทียมสับ	1 ช้อนชา
พริกไทยป่น	1/2 ช้อนชา
น้ำปลา	2-3 ช้อนโต๊ะ
น้ำซุปหรือน้ำ	5 ถ้วย
น้ำมัน	4 ช้อนโต๊ะ

วิธีทำ

1. น้ำซุปตั้งไฟ พอเดือด ถ้าต้องการใส่หมูสับให้ใส่เมื่อน้ำเดือด
2. เจียวไข่ให้เหลืองกรอบ เขี่ยไว้ข้างกระทะ ใส่กระเทียม เจียวให้เหลืองหอม สับไข่เป็นชิ้น ๆ ตักใส่หม้อน้ำซุป พอเดือด ใส่น้ำปลา
3. รองผักกาดหอมก้นถ้วย ตักแกงจืดไข่เจียวใส่ก้นถ้วย โรยพริกไทย ผักชี ใส่ตังฉ่าย เสิร์ฟร้อน ๆ

Tom Yam Pla Ka-phong Khao

Sour and spicy sea perch soup

ต้มยำปลากะพงขาว

Ingredients

1 sea perch weighing 500 grams
100 grams rice-straw mushrooms, slices in half
1 stem of lemon grass, crushed and cut into short pieces
5 slices of galangal
10 crushed hot chillies
4 crushed shallots
5 kaffir lime leaves
1 coriander plant
2 tbsp. lime juice
1 tbsp. fish sauce
3 cups water

Preparation

1. Scale, clean, and wash the fish and cut into pieces.
2. Place the water in a pot over medium heat and add the lemon grass, shallots, kaffir lime leaves torn into pieces, galangal, and chillies.
3. When the water has come to a good boil, add the fish and the mushrooms.
4. Add fish sauce and lime juice to taste, sprinkle with coriander greens, and serve hot.

เครื่องปรุง

ปลากะพงขาว น้ำหนัก 500 กรัม	1	ตัว
เห็ดฟางผ่าครึ่ง	100	กรัม
ตะไคร้ทุบหั่นท่อนสั้น	1	ต้น
ข่า	5	แว่น
พริกขี้หนูทุบ	10	เม็ด
หอมแดงทุบ	4	หัว
ใบมะกรูด	5	ใบ
ผักชี	1	ต้น
น้ำมะนาว	2	ช้อนโต๊ะ
น้ำปลา	1	ช้อนโต๊ะ
น้ำ	3	ถ้วย

วิธีทำ

1. ขอดเกล็ดปลากะพง ควักไส้ออก ล้างให้สะอาด หั่นเป็นชิ้น ๆ
2. ใส่น้ำลงในหม้อ ใช้ไฟกลาง ใส่ตะไคร้ หอมแดง ใบมะกรูดฉีก ข่า พริกขี้หนู
3. พอน้ำเดือดได้ที่ ใส่ปลาที่หั่นเตรียมไว้ ใส่เห็ดฟาง
4. ปรุงรสด้วยน้ำปลา น้ำมะนาว โรยผักชี รับประทานร้อน ๆ

Pla Chon Non Ple

Steamed serpent-head in sour and spicy soup

ปลาช่อนนอนเปล

Ingredients

1 serpent-head fish weighing 600-700 grams
1 large lemon grass stem, cut into lengths
5 disk-shaped slices of galangal
4 kaffir lime leaves, torn
5 cherry tomatoes, sliced in half lengthwise
1 tbsp. chopped phak chi fa-rang
15 hot chillies, broken open
5 roasted shallots, crushed
5 tbsp. tamarind juice
5 tbsp. fish sauce
4 cups soup stock

Preparation

1. Scale the serpent-head. Slice down the back and remove the backbone. Wash well, steam until the fish is done, and set aside.
2. Pour the stock into a pot and bring to a boil. Put in the lemon grass, galangal, fish sauce, and tamarind juice, allow to boil for a time, add the tomatoes, shallots, kaffir lime leaves, and chillies, and then remove from the heat.
3. Lay the steamed serpent-head in a long shallow bowl, pour the soup over it, sprinkle with phak chi fa-rang, and serve hot.

เครื่องปรุง

ปลาช่อน น้ำหนัก 600-700 กรัม	1 ตัว
ตะไคร้หั่นเป็นท่อน	1 ต้นใหญ่
ข่า	5 แว่น
ใบมะกรูดฉีก	4 ใบ
มะเขือเทศสีดาผ่าซีก	5 ลูก
ผักชีฝรั่งหั่น	1 ช้อนโต๊ะ
พริกขี้หนูบุบพอแตก	15 เม็ด
หอมแดงเผาบุบพอแตก	5 หัว
น้ำมะขามเปียก	5 ช้อนโต๊ะ
น้ำปลา	5 ช้อนโต๊ะ
น้ำซุป	4 ถ้วย

วิธีทำ

1. ขอดเกล็ดปลาช่อน ผ่ากลางตัว เอาก้างกลางออก ล้างให้สะอาด แล้วนำไปนึ่งให้สุก พักไว้
2. ตั้งหม้อใส่น้ำซุป ต้มให้เดือด ใส่ตะไคร้ ข่า น้ำปลา น้ำมะขามเปียก พอเดือดสักครู่ ใส่มะเขือเทศ หอมเผา ใบมะกรูด พริกขี้หนู ยกลง
3. นำตัวปลาช่อนที่เตรียมไว้ใส่ในชามเปล เอาน้ำที่ปรุงไว้ราดลงบนตัวปลา โรยผักชีฝรั่งหั่น รับประทานร้อน ๆ

Pla Tom Khem

Boiled mackerel steak

ปลาต้มเค็ม

Ingredients

500 grams one-half-inch thick Spanish mackerel steak
1 tbsp. chopped coriander root
5 garlic cloves
1 tsp. sugar
2 tsp. salt
2 tsp. sweet dark soy sauce
1 tbsp. lime juice
2 cups water
1 tbsp. cooking oil

Preparation

1. Dry the mackerel steak by wiping with absorbent paper, and then rub all surfaces with lime juice.
2. Pound the coriander root and garlic until finely ground.
3. In a wok, stir fry the pounded coriander root and garlic until fragrant, add the mackerel steak, fry until the flesh starts to shrink, and then add the soy sauce, salt, and sugar.
4. Transfer the contents of the wok to a pot, add the water, and simmer over low heat until the fish is tender and has absorbed the flavors of the soup.
5. Dip out onto a serving bowl, sprinkle with the coriander leaves.

เครื่องปรุง

ปลาอินทรีหั่นเป็นแว่นหนา ๑/๒ นิ้ว	๕๐๐ กรัม
รากผักชีหั่น	๑ ช้อนโต๊ะ
กระเทียม	๕ กลีบ
น้ำตาลทราย	๑ ช้อนชา
เกลือป่น	๒ ช้อนชา
ซีอิ๊วดำ	๒ ช้อนชา
น้ำมะนาว	๑ ช้อนโต๊ะ
น้ำ	๒ ถ้วย
น้ำมัน	๑ ช้อนโต๊ะ

วิธีทำ

1. ซับปลาให้แห้ง ทาด้วยน้ำมะนาว
2. โขลกรากผักชี และกระเทียมให้ละเอียด
3. ผัดรากผักชีและกระเทียมให้หอม ใส่ปลา ผัดพอปลาตึงตัว ใส่ซีอิ๊วดำ เกลือ น้ำตาล
4. ตักใส่หม้อ ใส่น้ำ ตั้งไฟอ่อน เคี่ยวให้ปลานุ่มและเครื่องปรุงเข้าถึงข้างในชิ้นปลาทั่ว
5. ตักใส่ถ้วย โรยผักชี เสิร์ฟ

Phat Neua Ka-thi

Dried beef in coconut milk

ผัดเนื้อกะทิ

Ingredients

200 grams salted dried beef
7 sliced shallots
1 1/2 cups coconut milk

Preparation

1. Select bright-red, lean, corded dried beef, wash, and roast until done. Next, pound the beef to separate the fibers and then tear into shreds.
2. Heat the coconut milk in a wok, add the beef, and stir with a spatula. Taste, and if desired, add salt and sugar.
3. When the coconut milk has thickened and coats the meat nicely, add the shallots, stir to mix everything together, and then remove from the heat.

เครื่องปรุง

เนื้อเค็ม	200	กรัม
หอมแดงซอย	7	หัว
หัวกะทิ	1 1/2	ถ้วย

วิธีทำ

1. เลือกเนื้อเค็มที่เป็นเส้นแดง ๆ ล้างน้ำแล้วนำไปปิ้งไฟให้สุก ทุบเนื้อให้แตกแล้วฉีกเป็นฝอย ๆ
2. ตั้งกระทะใส่กะทิ ผสมเนื้อลงไปผัดด้วยกัน ชิมดู ถ้าเนื้อไม่เค็มโรยเกลือเล็กน้อย และถ้าชอบหวานโรยน้ำตาลทรายเพิ่มได้
3. พอผัดจนน้ำกะทิงวดลงจับเนื้อแล้ว ใส่หอมลงผัดจนเข้ากันดี ยกลง

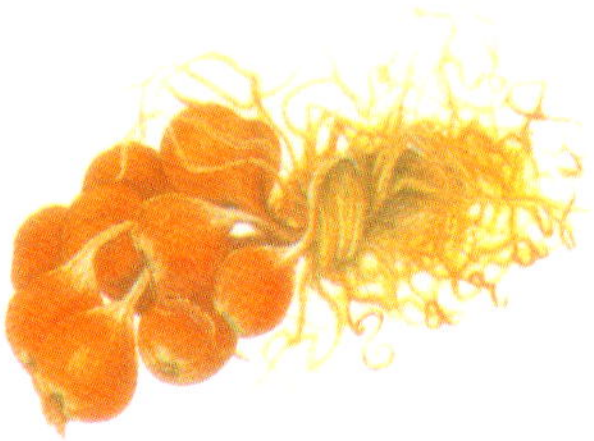

Kung Phat Wan

Sweet prawns

กุ้งผัดหวาน

Ingredients

500 grams white prawns
1 tbsp. salt
5 tbsp. sugar
4 tbsp. water

Preparation

1. Wash the prawns thoroughly, cut off the feelers, and set aside in a colander to drain.
2. Heat the water in a wok and add the salt and sugar. When the water has come to a boil and the sugar and salt have dissolved, add the prawns and stir continuously. When dry, remove from the wok.
3. Serve with lettuce, carrot and cabbage.

เครื่องปรุง

กุ้งชีแฮ้ขนาดกลาง	๕๐๐ กรัม
เกลือป่น	๑ ช้อนโต๊ะ
น้ำตาลทราย	๕ ช้อนโต๊ะ
น้ำ	๔ ช้อนโต๊ะ

วิธีทำ

1. ล้างกุ้งให้สะอาด ตัดหนวดกุ้งที่ยาวรุงรังออก ใส่กระชอนพักไว้
2. ใส่น้ำลงในกระทะ ใส่เกลือ น้ำตาล พอน้ำเดือด น้ำตาล เกลือละลายดีแล้ว ใส่กุ้งลงผัดจนน้ำแห้ง ตักขึ้น
3. เสิร์ฟกับผักกาดหอม แครอท และกะหล่ำปลี

Ma-Kheua Thet Phat Khai

Stir-fried tomato and egg

มะเขือเทศผัดไข่

Ingredients

2 tomatoes
4 bell chillies
2 eggs
1 tbsp. chopped garlic
1/2 tbsp. sugar
1-2 tbsp. fish sauce
2 tbsp. cooking oil

Preparation

1. Wash the tomatoes and cut into one-half-centimeter-thick slices.
2. Wash the bell chillies, slit open and remove and discard the insides, and then slice lengthwise.
3. Break the eggs into a bowl, add one-half teaspoonful of fish sauce, and beat.
4. Heat the oil in a wok. When hot, stir fry the garlic until fragrant and then add the bell chillies and stir fry a few moments. Now, add the tomato, fish sauce, and sugar and stir to mix.
5. Pour the egg into the wok and spread and scrape it around with the spatula. Turn the tomatoes over onto the egg. When the egg is done, dip out onto a plate and serve.

เครื่องปรุง

มะเขือเทศ	๒ ลูก
พริกหยวก	๔ เม็ด
ไข่	๒ ฟอง
กระเทียมสับ	๑ ช้อนโต๊ะ
น้ำตาลทราย	๑/๒ ช้อนโต๊ะ
น้ำปลา	๑-๒ ช้อนโต๊ะ
น้ำมัน	๒ ช้อนโต๊ะ

วิธีทำ

1. ล้างมะเขือเทศ หั่นเป็นแว่นหนา 1/2 ซม.
2. ล้างพริกหยวก ผ่ากลางแคะไส้ทิ้ง หั่นตามยาว
3. ต่อยไข่ใส่ชาม ใส่น้ำปลา 1 ช้อนชา ตีให้เข้ากัน
4. ใส่น้ำมันในกระทะ ตั้งไฟให้ร้อน ใส่กระเทียม เจียวพอหอม ใส่พริก ผัดสักครู่ ใส่มะเขือเทศ ใส่น้ำปลา น้ำตาล ผัดให้เข้ากัน
5. เทไข่ใส่กระทะ เกลี่ยให้ทั่ว กลับมะเขือเทศมาทับกับไข่ ไข่สุกตักขึ้น เสิร์ฟร้อน ๆ

Phak Kha-na Phat Tap

Stir-fried liver and kale

ผักคะน้าผัดตับ

Ingredients

2 large Chinese kale plants
100 grams pork liver
1/2 tbsp. light soy sauce
1 tbsp. oyster sauce
1/2 tbsp. fish sauce
3 tbsp. soup stock
3 tbsp. cooking oil

Preparation

1. Wash the kale, remove the tough outer part of the stems, and cut into 2-inch lengths.
2. Wash the liver and slice into bite-size pieces.
3. Heat the oil in a wok. When it is hot, stir fry the kale, liver, and stock.
4. Add soy sauce, oyster sauce, fish sauce to taste and continue frying until the liver is done.

Note : Be careful not to overcook ; this will make the liver tough.

เครื่องปรุง

ผักคะน้าต้นใหญ่	2	ต้น
ตับหมู	100	กรัม
ซีอิ๊วขาว	1/2	ช้อนโต๊ะ
น้ำมันหอย	1	ช้อนโต๊ะ
น้ำปลา	1/2	ช้อนโต๊ะ
น้ำซุป	3	ช้อนโต๊ะ
น้ำมัน	3	ช้อนโต๊ะ

วิธีทำ

1. ล้างผักคะน้าปอกเปลือกส่วนแข็งของลำต้นออก หั่นตามขวางขนาด 2 นิ้ว
2. ล้างตับหมู หั่นชิ้นพอคำ
3. ใส่น้ำมันในกระทะ ตั้งไฟให้ร้อน ใส่ผักคะน้า ใส่น้ำซุป ตับ
4. ปรุงรสด้วยซีอิ๊วขาว น้ำมันหอย น้ำปลา ผัด พอตับสุก ปิดไฟ

หมายเหตุ อย่าผัดนานจะทำให้ตับแข็ง ไม่อร่อย

Pu Phat Nam Phrik Phao

Stir-fried crab with roasted chilli paste

ปูผัดน้ำพริกเผา

Ingredients

2 serrated crabs
50 grams two-inch lengths of spring onion
5 red spur chillies sliced diagonally
5 crushed garlic cloves
2 1/2 tbsp. roasted chilli paste
1 tbsp. light soy sauce
1 tbsp. oyster sauce
1/2 cup soup stock
3 tbsp. cooking oil

Preparation

1. Clean and wash the crabs. Cut the bodies into quarters ; crack the claws.
2. Heat the oil in a wok. When hot, fry the garlic and spur chilli, and when fragrant, add the crab and stock and continue stir frying until the crab is done.
3. Add the roasted chilli paste and the soy sauce and oyster sauces, stir to mix thoroughly, add the spring onion, and remove from heat.

เครื่องปรุง

ปูทะเล	๒ ตัว
ต้นหอมหั่นท่อนยาว	
๒ นิ้ว	๕๐ กรัม
พริกชี้ฟ้าแดงหั่นเฉียง	๕ เม็ด
กระเทียมบุบ	๕ กลีบ
น้ำพริกเผา	๒ 1/๒ ช้อนโต๊ะ
ซีอิ๊วขาว	๑ ช้อนโต๊ะ
น้ำมันหอย	๑ ช้อนโต๊ะ
น้ำซุป	1/๒ ถ้วย
น้ำมัน	๓ ช้อนโต๊ะ

วิธีทำ

1. นำปูมาแกะกระดอง ล้างให้สะอาด สับเป็นสี่ชิ้น ทุบก้ามปู
2. ใส่น้ำมันในกระทะ ตั้งไฟให้ร้อน ใส่กระเทียม พริกชี้ฟ้า เจียวให้หอม ใส่ปู และน้ำซุป ผัดให้ทั่วจนปูสุก
3. ใส่น้ำพริกเผา ซีอิ๊วขาว น้ำมันหอย ผัดให้เข้ากัน ใส่ต้นหอม ปิดไฟ

Pla Kao Phat Ton Kra-thiam

Grouper stir-fried with garlic plant

ปลาเก๋าผัดต้นกระเทียม

Ingredients

200 grams thick pieces of grouper or sea perch meat
1 large garlic plant, sliced diagonally into sections
1 tsp. corn starch mixed with 1 tbsp. of water
1 tsp. whisky
2 tsp. oyster sauce
1 tbsp. light soy sauce
1/4 cup soup stock
3 tbsp. cooking oil

Preparation

1. Heat the oil in a wok. When hot, stir fry the fish. Add the stock, and when the fish is done, add the garlic plant.
2. Add oyster sauce, light soy sauce and whisky to taste. Add the corn starch and water mixture. Taste and season additionally if desired. Dip out onto a platter and serve hot.

เครื่องปรุง

เนื้อปลาเก๋า หรือปลากะพงขาว หั่นชิ้นหนา	200	กรัม
ต้นกระเทียมใหญ่หั่นเฉียง	1	ต้น
แป้งข้าวโพด (ละลายน้ำ 1 ช้อนโต๊ะ)	1	ช้อนชา
วิสกี้	1	ช้อนชา
น้ำมันหอย	2	ช้อนโต๊ะ
ซีอิ๊วขาว	1	ช้อนโต๊ะ
น้ำซุป	1/4	ถ้วย
น้ำมัน	3	ช้อนโต๊ะ

วิธีทำ

1. ใส่น้ำมันในกระทะ พอน้ำมันร้อนใส่ปลาลงผัด เติมน้ำซุป เมื่อปลาสุกใส่ต้นกระเทียม
2. ปรุงรสด้วยน้ำมันหอย ซีอิ๊วขาว วิสกี้ ใส่แป้งข้าวโพด ผัดให้เข้ากัน ชิมรส ตักใส่จาน เสิร์ฟร้อน ๆ

Phak Kra-chet Na Kai

Stir-fried water mimosa with ground chicken

ผักกระเฉดหน้าไก่

Ingredients

2 cups tender young water mimosa tips
cut 3-inches long
100 grams ground chicken meat
10 hot chillies
10 garlic cloves
1 tbsp. light soy sauce
1/2 tbsp. fermented soybeans
1 tbsp. oyster sauce
3 tbsp. cooking oil

Preparation

1. Pound the garlic and chillies.
2. Heat two tablespoonsful of the oil in a wok until very hot. Add the water mimosa sprinkle with water, and fry over high heat, stirring vigorously ; then, dip out onto a platter.
3. Heat the oil in a wok. When hot, fry the pounded garlic and chillies. When fragrant, add the chicken, fermented soybeans, oyster sauce, and soy sauce. Continue stir frying until done ; then dip out over the water mimosa.

เครื่องปรุง

ผักกระเฉดอ่อน เด็ดยาว 3 นิ้ว	2 ถ้วย
ไก่สับ	100 กรัม
พริกขี้หนู	10 เม็ด
กระเทียม	10 กลีบ
ซีอิ๊วขาว	1 ช้อนโต๊ะ
เต้าเจี้ยว	1/2 ช้อนโต๊ะ
น้ำมันหอย	1 ช้อนโต๊ะ
น้ำมัน	3 ช้อนโต๊ะ

วิธีทำ

1. โขลกกระเทียมกับพริกขี้หนู
2. ใส่น้ำมัน 2 ช้อนโต๊ะ ลงในกระทะ ตั้งไฟให้ร้อนจัด ใส่ผักกระเฉด พรมน้ำ ผัดไฟแรง เร็ว ๆ ตักใส่จาน
3. ใส่น้ำมันที่เหลือลงในกระทะ พอร้อนใส่เครื่องที่โขลกไว้ เจียวพอหอม ใส่ไก่ เต้าเจี้ยว ซีอิ๊ว-ขาว น้ำมันหอย ผัดให้เข้ากัน ตักราดบนผักกระเฉดที่ใส่จานไว้

Phak Bung Na Mu

Stir-fried swamp cabbage with ground pork

ผักบุ้งหน้าหมู

Ingredients

2 cups tender young swamp cabbage tips cut 3-inches long
100 grams ground pork
10 hot chillies
5 garlic cloves
1 tbsp. light soy sauce
1/2 tbsp. fermented soybeans
1 tbsp. oyster sauce
3 tbsp. cooking oil

Preparation

1. Pound the garlic and the hot chillies.
2. Heat two tablespoonful of the oil in a wok until very hot. Add the swamp cabbage, sprinkle with water, and fry over high heat, stirring vigorously ; then, dip out onto a platter.
3. Heat the remaining oil in a wok. When hot, add the pounded garlic and chilli. When fragrant, add the pork, fermented soybeans, and oyster and soy sauce. Mix well, and when ready, dip out over the swamp cabbage.

เครื่องปรุง

ผักบุ้งอ่อน เด็ดยาว ๓ นิ้ว	๒	ถ้วย
หมูสับ	๑๐๐	กรัม
พริกขี้หนู	๑๐	เม็ด
กระเทียม	๕	กลีบ
ซีอิ๊วขาว	๑	ช้อนโต๊ะ
เต้าเจี้ยว	๑/๒	ช้อนโต๊ะ
น้ำมันหอย	๑	ช้อนโต๊ะ
น้ำมัน	๓	ช้อนโต๊ะ

วิธีทำ

1. โขลกกระเทียมกับพริกขี้หนู
2. ใส่น้ำมัน 2 ช้อนโต๊ะ ลงในกระทะ ตั้งไฟให้ร้อนจัด ใส่ผักบุ้ง พรมน้ำ ผัดไฟแรงเร็ว ๆ ตักใส่จาน
3. ใส่น้ำมันที่เหลือลงในกระทะ พอร้อนใส่เครื่องที่โขลกไว้ เจียวพอหอม ใส่หมูสับ เต้าเจี้ยว ซีอิ๊วขาว น้ำมันหอย ผัดให้เข้ากัน ตักราดบนผักบุ้งที่เตรียมไว้

Thua Lan Tao Phat Kung

Stir-fried prawns and snow peas

ถั่วลันเตาผัดกุ้ง

Ingredients

200 grams snow peas
100 grams prawns
2 garlic plants
5 crushed garlic cloves
2 tbsp. light soy sauce
3 tbsp. soup stock
3 tbsp. cooking oil

Preparation

1. Wash the snow peas and remove the strings from the pods.
2. Wash the garlic plants and cut into 3-inch lengths.
3. Wash, shell, and devein the prawns, leaving the tails in place.
4. Heat the oil in a wok. When hot, fry the garlic until fragrant ; next, add the snow peas and stock, stir fry for a short while, and then add the prawns.
5. Add soy sauce to taste, stir to mix, add the garlic plants, and when everything is done, remove from the heat.

เครื่องปรุง

ถั่วลันเตา	๒๐๐ กรัม
กุ้งสด	๑๐๐ กรัม
ต้นกระเทียม	๒ ต้น
กระเทียมบุบ	๕ กลีบ
ซีอิ๊วขาว	๒ ช้อนโต๊ะ
น้ำซุป	๓ ช้อนโต๊ะ
น้ำมัน	๓ ช้อนโต๊ะ

วิธีทำ

1. ล้างถั่วลันเตา ดึงเส้นข้างที่แข็งออก
2. ล้างต้นกระเทียม หั่นยาว 3 นิ้ว
3. ล้างกุ้งให้สะอาด ปอกเปลือกตัดหัวไว้หาง ผ่าหลังชักเส้นดำออก
4. ใส่น้ำมันลงในกระทะ ตั้งไฟให้ร้อน ใส่กระเทียมเจียวพอหอม ใส่ถั่วลันเตา น้ำซุป ผัดสักครู่ ใส่กุ้ง
5. ปรุงรสด้วยซีอิ๊วขาว ผัดให้เข้ากัน ใส่ต้นกระ-เทียม สุกทั่ว ปิดไฟ

Buap Phat Kung

Stir-fried prawns and sponge gourd

บวบผัดกุ้ง

Ingredients

500 grams angled sponge gourd
200 grams white prawns
4 crushed garlic cloves
1/2 tbsp. light soy sauce
1 tbsp. oyster sauce
1/2 tbsp. fish sauce
3 tbsp. soup stock
3 tbsp. cooking oil

Preparation

1. Peel the gourd, wash, and cut diagonally into bite-size pieces.
2. Wash, shell, and devein the prawns, leaving the tails on.
3. Heat the oil in a wok. When hot, add the garlic, stir fry a short while, add the gourd, and continue stir frying.
4. Add the fish sauce, soy sauce, oyster sauce, and stock, stir to mix everything well, add the prawns, and continue stir frying. When the prawns are done, turn off the heat.

เครื่องปรุง

บวบเหลี่ยม	500 กรัม
กุ้งชีแฮ้	200 กรัม
กระเทียมบุบ	4 กลีบ
ซีอิ๊วขาว	1/2 ช้อนโต๊ะ
น้ำมันหอย	1 ช้อนโต๊ะ
น้ำปลา	1/2 ช้อนโต๊ะ
น้ำซุป	3 ช้อนโต๊ะ
น้ำมัน	3 ช้อนโต๊ะ

วิธีทำ

1. ปอกเปลือกบวบออก ล้างให้สะอาด หั่นเฉียงพอคำ
2. ปอกเปลือกกุ้ง ตัดหัวไว้หาง ผ่าหลังชักเส้นดำออก
3. ใส่น้ำมันลงในกระทะ ตั้งไฟให้ร้อน ใส่กระเทียมเจียวพอหอม ใส่บวบลงผัด
4. ปรุงรสด้วยน้ำปลา ซีอิ๊วขาว น้ำมันหอย น้ำซุป ผัดให้ทั่ว ใส่กุ้ง สักครู่กุ้งสุก ปิดไฟ

Printed in Thailand

Publisher and Distributor Sangdad Publishing Co.,Ltd.

320 Lat Phrao 94 (Town in Town), Wongthonglang, Bangkok 10310

Tel. (662) 538-7576, 538-5553, 934-4411

Fax: (662) 538-1499